Lord, It Was You:
Poetry & Wisdom

Crystal Wilson-Honesty

Table of Contents

Epiphany

As I reflected on our 2005 Women's Ministry Retreat, something came to me with such clarity that I was almost floored. I had been praying for guidance and direction with respect to my vocation within the church. For many years my statement has been that I did not want the responsibility that goes along with my gifts. In actuality, I was not running from the responsibility, I was running from myself because I did not believe in my gifts. I did not believe that I had what it took to do God's work and do it well.

If you do not acknowledge, accept and utilize your gifts, you are doing yourself a great disservice and you are not honoring God for the things that he has given you.

Having this moment of clarity made me feel better about myself, the gifts that God has given me and has given me the courage to say Lord, I am ready now.

God has given me the gift of a song. I will sing praises to His name.
God has given me the gift of words. I will write things to glorify Him.
God has given me a spirit of helps. I will do my best to serve Him and His people.

When I first started to write the poems and prayers that follow, I had no idea what God had in store for me, but I knew that as he gave me the words, I had to write them down. There was not going to be an introduction, just the things that he placed on my heart to write. But it was placed on my heart to write down my moment of clarity and what it meant to me.

I used to say that I only wrote when I was depressed. God told me to go back and look at some of my previous work. In looking at my work from the 1980's and the 1990's, I found that it was not depressing at all, but very encouraging, so I have decided to include some of those works with the new things that God has given me and I pray that there is more to come.

Letter to my Father

Through all my tribulations
Through my stress and strife
I know God has a plan
For my life

No pain or illness
No debt incurred
Can deter me from
The God I serve

For you are always doing
Great things for me
All I must do is
Have faith and believe

See when I get down and out
And I get confused
I know it's time for me
To get closer to you

I know that if I pray
And listen for your voice
You will always help me
To make the right choice

Can't go by what I see
Or even what I've heard
The only way to be sure
Is to read your word

When I am trapped in darkness
Not knowing left from right
You are always there
Lord, You are my light

You see, no matter what happens
I know in the end
Having you in my life
Is how I can win

See I didn't come this far
All by myself
You have always been here
To be my help

So as your child
In everything that I do
I only want to bring
Glory to you

I want to say I love you Father
From my very depths
I'm so glad I got to know you
For myself

And I want to say thank you Father
For always keeping me safe
Nothing will separate me
From my faith

And though at times faith gets shaken

I still hold onto your hand
For I know that you have
The master plan

And all things work for the good
Of them who love you
And I praise your name Father
For everything that you do

Submitting to His Will

I want to live my life
As a testament to you
Submitting to your will Lord
Is all I want to do

I am just a sinner
Falling short of your grace
I want nothing to prevent me
From someday seeing your face

I will always do my best
To live in a Christian way
I will seek you out Lord
Each and every day

I know you have a plan
And I know your word is true
Submitting to your will Lord
Is all I want to do

Life only gets harder
When you're trying to live right
But with you I have the victory
I can win the fight

The more I seek you out Lord
The stronger temptation gets
But all I need is your love

For it's the best thing yet

I get such peace Lord
From spending time with you
Submitting to your will Lord
Is all I want to do

In time you will reveal
What you have in store for me
So I make room in my heart, Lord
More availability

I will listen for your voice Lord
I'll incline my ear to hear
I will be still and wait Lord
So your message will be clear

I will obey your word Lord
For your word is tried and true
Submitting to your will Lord
Is all I want to do

Conversation with My Father

Sometimes when I'm going through
And my spirit is on the ground
I look for help in people
And no one can be found

Sometimes my heart gets broken
And I don't know what to do
In those moments I know
That I should turn to you

But like your children sometimes do
I try to handle it alone
But you came to me and told me
Something I have always known

You said I am the Lord, your Father
And you are still my child
You need to come into my house
And talk to me for a while

You said I'll always love and protect you
Even when you're doing wrong
I'll never turn my back on you
I'll never leave you alone

You told me in your time of struggle child
You need only to call on me
My help is greater than any other

Try for yourself, and you will see

All I ask is that you obey child
And live according to my will

And while you wait for me to lead you
I command you to be still

Wait for my instruction
And act according to my word
When I receive the glory
I'll know that I've been heard

I want to thank you Father
For giving your advice
For loving me in spite of me
For being the center of my life

I'll live my life to please you
I'll try not to let you down
And I know that when I need you
I should just kneel on the ground

I know that if I wait, Lord
That you will be right there
And for this I praise your name Father
Because I know I'm in your care

Thank you Holy Father
For being God all by yourself
For providing every need Lord
When I have no one else

Thank you for reminding me
To whom I belong
My desire to be closer to you
Is now so very strong

Just the mention of your name Lord
Makes my soul smile
Thanks for being my Father
And for letting me be your child.

Peace Within

Peace within
Peace within
Everyday Lord you are
My peace within

Lord your children need you
Our world is full of grief and pain
We need only to watch the news
To hear of more people slain
The enemy is strong Lord
And many don't know how to fight
Please guide them along your path Lord
Help them to walk in your light

Please give them peace within
Peace within
Everyday Lord you are
My peace within

Lord, please watch over our babies
The future leaders of our world
Help us learn to nurture and love them
Keep them safe from the turmoil
Lord let them grow in wisdom
From those who have gone on before
Teach them that life is not about
How to settle the next score
Show them peace within

Peace within
Everyday Lord you are
My peace within

Lord protect our elders
Let them be happy in their golden years
Teach their children to cherish them
Allow them to rest easy with no fears
Lord they have paved the way
For everything that we now do
One thing they always tried to teach us
Is to put our faith in you

May they have peace within
Peace within
Everyday Lord you are
My peace within

With all of the horror
Surrounding us everyday
I am so blessed to have you
So glad that I am able to say
That I have peace within
Peace within
Thank you Lord for being
My peace within

The Heart Speaks Volumes

If I could look inside your heart, what would I see?
Would there be love and kindness?
Nurturing and caring?
Purity and genuine concern for mankind?

Would it reflect the things that you say?
That you love your neighbor, brother, friend?
Or would it prove that your actions speak louder
Than your actual behavior?

Would it show me strength of character, or false
bravado?
Would it show that you are being true to yourself?
Or that you are pretending to be something you aren't
Just to please the masses?

If you could look inside my heart, what would you want
to see?
Someone who can be a living witness of what it is to
Walk the Christian walk and talk the Christian talk
Not only while in church but in everything they do?

Someone who lives their life to do God's work
Not only when it is convenient but also when it's not?
Someone who is charitable to those less fortunate
always
Not when just promoting a cause?

Someone whose spirit is so bright that it can be seen
By anyone who happens to be in their presence?
Or someone who changes who they are
By the company that they are in?

When God looks into our hearts what does he see?
Someone who praises him through the good and bad
times?
Or someone who only acknowledges him when
everything
Is going their way?

Will he see a Christian of convenience or a Christian of
substance?
Someone willing to be available to him in mind, body
and spirit
Or one of those recognition Christians acting out their
selfish need
To be seen, honored and praised?
What does your heart say about you?

Your Servant's Prayer

Can you hear your children Father?
They are crying out in pain
They're being hurt by the world
And are calling out your name

Can you see them Father?
Their eyes shining with tears
For fear of not being forgiven
For all of their wrongdoing years

Can you feel them Father?
Their hearts are burning within
With desire to walk with you
And turn away from sin

Can you speak to their hearts Father?
Let them know you are a God of Love
Tell them that you grant them grace
From your throne above

Will you grant them peace Father?
And provide them the state of mind
That you alone are their salvation
No better friend will they find

Now will you bless them Father?
Provide their needs each day
Let them know when darkness comes

That you will light the way

I know that if you do these things
They will bless and praise your name
For you have done these things for me
And my life you have changed

So I am asking you Father
This is your servant's prayer
Please hear the cries of you children
Enable them to know you are there

Request for Blessings

God, bless the single mother
Working hard to make ends meet
Trying to provide clothes, food, and shelter
Keep her children off the street
Please keep her Lord
Show her how to pray
Help her seek your guidance Lord
Let her know you are the way

God, bless the troubled father
Working hard and getting nowhere
He has a wife and children
That you have placed in his care
Let him know you're there Lord
Help him to stay strong
Keep him focused on your path Lord
You'll never steer him wrong

God, bless the family
Trying hard to stay together
Let them know that with your help
There's no storm that they can't weather
Please keep them united Lord
Help them take pride in their history
Assure them that although there will be struggles
With you they can claim the victory
God, bless the children
Keep them out of harm's way

That they will grow to love and praise you
As their children will someday
Help them fight against the pressure
And temptations from their friends
Let them know that although they are with them today
It is you they must meet in the end
Amen

God Listens

I sit back and listen
To my children complain
Many of their issues
Seem to be the same

Lord, when will you bless me?
I try to avoid sin
When will you let me meet
Some decent men?

Why can't I get a job, Lord
With the degree that I've earned?
In everything I attempt
I always get burned

Everything I've accomplished
I've done all by myself
Never had to depend
On anyone else

As I listen to these children
While they tell their story
I have yet to hear them say
To God be the glory

In all they've accomplished
And think they've done by themselves
They have never acknowledged

The greatest source of their help

They want to get a job
With the degree that they've earned
With Me the lesson is taught
Until the lesson is learned

Their lives will get better
When their faith gets strong
When they know and understand
To whom they belong

I am the Father
The giver of all
The one whom when they stumbled
Did not let them fall

I have always been there
To supply their every need
Yet they fail to praise Me
By thought, word or deed.

When they decide to walk with Me
And to take my hand
When they realize the I
Have the master plan

I will listen to their pleas
And hear their prayers
Because I am here for them
To cast upon their cares

When they know that in all things
I deserve the glory
I know that they will tell
A very different story

They will tell of My mercy
And all of My goodness
They will speak of the many ways
In which their lives have been blessed

They will gladly acknowledge
That they are my child
Just the mention of my name
Will bring about a smile

They will tell everyone
The battle has been won
And they will praise Me
For the great things I have done

They will continue to praise me
Even when things are going bad
They will know Mine is the best love
That they've ever had

They will know that I have supplied
Each and every need
And they will show gratitude
By their thoughts, words and deeds

Lord, Hear My Plea

Lord, I come before you
Oh bended knee
With uplifted hands
Mine eyes to the sky
Crying out to you
I am your servant
Here am I, Lord
Use me to do your will

Lord, there are many
Who need your loving touch
To feel your presence
To hear your voice
To hear your word
Send me Lord
My cup is empty
Please fill me with your spirit

Lord, I know I am not worthy
To make this request of you
To speak to your people
On your behalf
To deliver your message
But I beseech you, O Lord
To see something in me
Worthy of being used

Lord, put a word on my tongue

A song in my heart
A glow in my spirit
Your will in my soul
Let people see you
When they look at me
One unworthy of all you give
Yet is pleading to do your work

Lord I am but a sinner
Pleading to do your service
Desiring to do your will
Wanting to serve your people
In a manner pleasing to you
I am an empty vessel
Waiting to be filled by you
And spread your love and joy
Please Father, hear my plea

I Praise You, Lord

I praise you Lord
Through the good times
And ones that are tough
I praise you Lord
When the going gets rough

I praise you Lord
For I am nothing
Without you
I praise you Lord
For your word is true

I praise you Lord
Even when I feel as though
I am all alone
I praise you Lord
For the love you have shown

I praise you Lord
When I am sick
Or in pain
I praise you Lord
For always being the same

I praise you Lord
When my children
Just won't behave
I praise you Lord

For their souls You will save

I praise you Lord
When my friends turn
Their backs on me
I praise you Lord
I put my faith in Thee

I praise you Lord
When my struggles seem
Too much to bear
I praise you Lord
I know I am in your care

I praise you Lord
It doesn't matter
How far I fall
I praise you Lord
My name you still call

I praise you Lord
For cloudy days
When there is no sun
I praise you Lord
For the great things you've done

I praise you Lord
When the skies are
Clear and blue
I praise you Lord
For all you still do

Thank You Lord

Are you listening Lord?
It's me again, your humble servant
I just had to take a moment to say
Thank you.

When I was young and even not so young
And placed myself in dangerous situations
You brought me through them safely
For that Lord, I thank you

When my bills and rent were due
And I did not have a job
You kept your word and supplied my needs
For that Lord, I thank you

When my body was in pain
And I had to have surgery
The problem was not serious
For that Lord, I thank you

When I go through a depression
And I come out it
Still in my right mind
For that Lord, I thank you

When I was involved with people
Who were clearly wrong for me
You revealed them to me and led me away

For that Lord, I thank you

When I was being willful and stubborn
You didn't turn your back on me
You loved me still
And for that Lord I have to
Drop to my knees
Bow my head
Close my eyes
Lift my hands
And say thank you

Lord, It Was You

When my innocence was being stolen
At the tender age of eight
An angel came down
Stopped the torture
And led me safely home
Lord, I know that it was you

When the gangs tried to recruit me
And wanted to do me bodily harm
Because I would not conform
I got home from school safely
Each and every day
Lord, I know that it was you

When peers tried to pressure me
Into doing things that I knew were wrong
I was able to stand my ground
Say no, that's not for me
Graduate high school with no real problems
Lord, I know that it was you

When I was able to get an apartment
Work two jobs while going to school
Keep the bills and rent paid
Keep food on the table
Not fall over from exhaustion
Lord, I know that it was you

When my friend stopped speaking to me
Because I was not ready to accept
What he wanted to offer me
And then he returned
And became my husband
Lord, I know that it was you

When a life growing inside of me
Was taken away in the womb
Because it was not strong enough
To survive in the outside world
I was able to have peace of mind
Lord, I know that it was you

When going through
The illness of pregnancy
The pain of labor
And giving birth to
Two beautiful, healthy children
Lord, I know that it was you

When my child was stolen
And in the care of strangers
She was returned safely
Clean and not hungry
No harm came to her
Lord, I know that it was you

When people placed in authority over me
Have made my life a living hell
I made a change in my attitude
To be able to work with them

And get the job done
Lord, I know that it was you

When my friend was taken
In the prime of his life
Because he was suffering
You saw fit to call him home
Though I miss him dearly
Lord, I know that it was you

When people have been placed in my life
The good ones have remained
And become great friends
The wrong ones were revealed
And subsequently removed
Lord, I know that it was you

Through all that I have endured
Whether good and pleasant
Or a learning experience
That I managed to survive
I know that I am better for them all
Lord, because it was you

The Wisdom of Our Foundation

The church where we stand today
And everything contained within
Was built upon the wisdom
Of our foundation

Their faith in God
And their selfless loyalty
Has made it possible for us
To come together in this place

They were part of the struggle
They were there for the fight
Which has given us the right
To come together in worship

Every tear that they have shed
And every drop of the their sweat
Has laid the foundation
For us to be here today

They wear beautiful crowns
Of gray, sliver and white
Upon glorious heads
Which contain our history

You see all around you
Many years of wisdom
And untold mystery

In every line etched in their faces

Look to them
As your example
Of the greatness
That you can become

Look to them
For the answers
To life's mysteries
Not found in a book

Look to them
Because God willing
One day they are who
We will become

Look to the wisdom
Of our Foundation
As an example of the strength it takes
To build a great nation

Look to the wisdom
Of our foundation
For their eyes have seen
More than we will ever know

Look to the wisdom of our foundation

God Sent Me A Man

God sent me a man
That fought for my attention
Vied for my affection
I didn't know his intentions
So I gave him much rejection

I didn't know that he was sent
To teach me a valuable lesson
About men and persuasion
About future relations
And about expectations

This young man and I
Were placed in a situation
Had a conversation
He got my attention
Spoke of his intentions

He made me realize that I
Was worthy of affection
Should set the limitations
In all situations
That dealt with my emotions

He showed me levels of love
Of the highest elevation
I felt such elation
Thanked God for my situation

For he deserved the recognition

And then...

God gave us a revelation
About our situation
That ended our relations
I felt such confusion
But knew there was a reason

Though I was heartbroken
I developed higher expectations
From men and relations
About protecting my emotions
From those with bad intentions

I know that I am worthy
Of love and affection
Caring and compassion
Love without limitation
Romance and passion

That man set the standard
For my current situation
Marriage with affection
No problems with rejection
Again God gets the recognition

Thank God for that man
And his art of persuasion
Which lead to the conversation
In which I learned the lesson

About love and devotion

Why?

Why is God so good to us
When we continue to abuse ourselves
And each other
To use people for our own selfish gain
And we treat Him just like we treat
So many others
Only call Him when we need something
Want something
Or if we are in trouble

Why does God continue to bless us
When we go out and repeatedly sin
Against Him and each other
Have no love for our brother
Or even one another
We lie, cheat and steal
Cause wounds that never heal
Act as though we cannot feel
The pain we cause those
That we claim to love

Why should God speak to our minds
Our hearts and spirits
When we refuse to listen
Or obey His word,
And when we refuse to do those things
That He is asking of us
Then have the unmitigated gall
To question his commands

Why does God continue to keep us
Safe from harmful and dangerous situations
And heal our hurts
Especially when we are the ones
Who place ourselves in predicaments
For unfortunate things
To happen to us

And why does God continue to love us

Unconditionally and passionately
When we can't even love ourselves
Or for that matter anyone else
Our lives become a total living hell
And we make everyone else
Around us miserable
Just because we have the
Inability to find happiness

The answer to these questions
Is very simple indeed
And so plain and direct
Yet easy to believe...
Because that is what a parent does
For their child

I Scream in Silence

I scream in silence
Through my inner pain
And my quiet tears
For the world won't understand
But I know my Father hears

I scream in silence
For the state of our world
For every life prematurely taken away
Through senseless acts of violence
Lord, please teach us to pray!

I scream in silence
Because no one seems to care
About our children and our elderly
Slipping away unnoticed
Heavenly Father, help us to see!

I scream in silence
Because Your children cannot live
In harmony with each other
Even though Your word dictates
That we are to love our brother

I scream in silence
Because I know that You have
Inclined Your ear to hear to hear my plea
And that change will be eminent
If we remain faithful and on bended knee

The Mirror

When you look into the mirror
Who do you see looking back at you?
Do you see yourself through the eyes of man?
Or through the eyes of the maker
Who created everything?

Do you see someone who can do
All things through Christ who strengthens you?
Or someone who is unwilling to fulfill their destiny
Because man has stated that who you are
Is not enough?

Do you see someone who can
Hold their head high and cry out
I am beautifully and wonderfully made
By the one who also created
The Heaven and Earth?

Or someone who lives their life
Looking down at the ground
Because the trials of everyday life
And the standards of man
Has depleted their self worth?

When you look in the mirror
And evaluate the image looking back at you
Strive to see yourself through the eyes
Of the one who made you and know
That His work is good.

What Will You Give Jesus for His Birthday?

Will you give him a promise
That you will follow him
As soon as you get your life in order?
Or will you let him order your steps?

Will you say to him
Lord, I can only give so much right now
But I will give you more tomorrow
And tomorrow never comes for you?

Will you offer Him
Who died on the cross for you
Only half of you when He is the one
Who gave his all for you?

Will you promise to worship Him
When the spirit moves you
Or will you let His spirit in
And carry Him with you at all times?

I ask you again... What will you give Jesus for His
Birthday?

Will you invite Him to your celebrations
Where He should be the guest of honor
Or forget that the season is about Him
And that all you have is because of His love?

Will you have faith enough in Him to believe

That no matter what comes your way
He is with you and that He
Can bring you safely out?

Will you offer Him hope
By teaching your children about Him
And showing them how to worship Him
That they may do the same for generations to follow?

What will you give Jesus for His birthday?

Will you give your all for Him
Just as he did for you?
Because all He truly wants
Is all of you.

God Is There For You

Whenever you are feeling down
And think you are at your wits end,
Whenever you feel things can't get worse
But then the do
I am here for you

When you feel that you are all alone
And that no one truly cares
Just take a look around
Somewhere you will find me
Waiting patiently

Waiting with a caring heart
And a strong shoulder to lean on
Ready to listen and not criticize
With open arms to embrace you
I am here for you

I will be here to remind you
That no matter how tough it gets
You are never alone
I will always be here
Ready, willing and able to care
Ready, willing and able to share

Whatever burden it seems
Life drops unto you
I am here to love and support you

Without unneeded pain
No matter what the problem may be
I am here for you

Learn to Love You

In life we are our own worst critics
Always harder on ourselves
Than anyone else
For the mistakes we have made

There are times when we don't
Care about ourselves
And we wonder why
Anyone else does

These are times
When we should realize that
As we are our own worst enemy
We must be our own best friend

We have to learn to appreciate ourselves
And accept that we may
Often fall short of the goal
That we've set for ourselves

We must understand that
It is not our plan that matters
But God's master plan
That we must ultimately follow

Once we have accomplished this
We can learn not only to like ourselves
But to love ourselves

And to better accept those who love us

We must learn to accept ourselves
For who we are we are and
Try to be the best person
That we know how
Life's Road

As I walk along this road
The road going nowhere
I am not alone
Pain and sorrow are my constant companions
Faithful friends who follow me
Wherever I go

Still traveling down this road
This road leading nowhere
Two strangers appear
Strangers called Friendship and Love
Accompanying me on my journey
We leave pain and sorrow behind

Now I travel a new road
A road going somewhere
Friendship and Love are at my side
We keep moving forward, never looking back
Not once remembering pain and sorrow
For they are now thing of the past

Think About It

Life is too short
To stand in one place
And let the whole world
Just pass you by

Unless that one place
That you are standing
Is where you choose to live
And where you choose to die

There is not enough time
To waste waiting
For everything and everyone
Around you to make a change

You must take the initiative
To make your life better
When times are hard
Your own life you must rearrange

You cannot keep hoping
That the future will be brighter
Unless you take the necessary steps
To help that hope along

Because one day you will wake up
The future will still be dim
And all your hopes and dreams

For a brighter future will be gone

Don't hold onto false promises
From another mortal being
That they can give you
A better tomorrow

For tomorrow is not promised
To any one of us
And all of their false promises
Will bring you pain and sorrow

A little word of wisdom
Please hear me when I say
Your hopes for a brighter tomorrow
Must begin with your living today

Think About It

In My Dreams

In my dreams
The world in which we live
Is beautiful, tranquil, warm
And a very peaceful place

In my dreams
People open up their arms
And their hearts to each other
Not slam doors in your face

In my dreams
There is no such thing
As a homeless person
Living on a cruel and brutal street

In my dreams
Children are not dying
From the disease of poverty
Lack of medication and good food to eat

In my dreams
War between countries
Simply does not exist
In everyone's heart there is peace

In my dreams
Racial tension and hatred
Has vanished from the world

And all violence has ceased

In my dreams
There is total equality
Between races and sexes
Men, women and children alike

In my dreams
We are naturally given
The rights and privileges
For which our ancestors had to fight

In my dreams
You don't step on people
And ruin my lives
Just to get ahead

In my dreams
The headlines don't read
Drugs and gangs are on the rise

More people found dead

Then I wake up!

Talking with Daddy

Have you ever been going through something and needed someone to talk to, and none of your family and friends were around for you?

Have you ever had something on your heart and mind that you didn't feel that you could trust another human being with?

Have you ever been in so much emotional distress and felt that you had no one to turn too?

Have you ever entrusted someone with something personal, only to find that they were more than willing to share your confidential information with any and everyone who would listen to them?

If we are truly honest with ourselves, each and every one of us could answer these questions in the affirmative. Many of us, if not all of us, have been disappointed when we entrusted our feelings and secrets to another human being. We discuss our situations with those who are as fallible as we are, and things don't get better, but often get worse.

When we are going through the trials and tribulations of our daily lives, we need to turn to the one who is incapable of letting us down. It is in these times that we need to have a conversation with the Father. By having a conversation with the Father, I mean having an open dialog which includes not only talking, but listening to the voice of God.

Although your friends and even your earthly parents can be source of advice, it may not be the advice you need for your situation. When you listen to the voice of the Father, he will never steer you wrong.

In order to hear the voice of the Father, we must be willing to listen with an inclined ear, for the voice of the Father will not be loud and booming, but may come as a whisper. Only those who are willing to hear it will hear it. God will speak to those who seek him out with their whole heart, mind and spirit.

The next time you have a situation and need someone to turn too, before you turn to those who may disappoint you, hasten to the throne of the Almighty and give your situation to Him. There may not be a need to speak to anyone else about it. While you are trying to figure out how to handle your situation, God has already resolved your issue and is waiting for you to come to Him for the answer. So, go to Him, talk to Him, listen to Him and He will bring you through.

Reflection of You

When you look at yourself in the mirror, how do you view yourself? Do you view yourself in a human perspective or a spiritual perspective?

How many of us have looked in the mirror and become depressed by the image looking back at us? Have you ever asked yourself why what you see is not pleasing in your sight? We are often not pleased by our reflection because mankind has put a stipulation on what is acceptable and what is not when it comes to appearance. Society has its standard about physical beauty and what it should look like and we tend to go out of our way to live up to the standards of society, often failing.

When you look at others, what do you see? Do you tend to form and opinion about a person simply based on their outward appearance? Realistically, we are all guilty of doing this at some point in our lives. We have shied away from a person on the street who appeared to be not as clean as we are, or those who have the appearance of someone that society deems undesirable.

If we are created in the image of God, when we look at ourselves, or others, we should see a reflection of God's love. We should see our Father in everyone that we come in contact with. Don't get me wrong, there are those who, even though God created them, are out to do

wrong. God has also blessed us with common sense and using common sense, we know whom we should make contact with, and whom we should not. Even if we don't always pay attention, the signs are there.
In looking at ourselves, and others, we should see the goodness of God and his love. We should see his light shine through us and be a light to those who are trapped in darkness. We should put aside our natural sight and use our spiritual sight and not form opinions about others based on physical attributes or attire. God would never do that to us, so who are we to do that to any of his children? The word of God states in Matthew 7:

1 "Do not judge, or you too will be judged.
2 For in the same way you judge others, you will be judged, and with the measure you use, it will be measured to you.
3 "Why do you look at the speck of sawdust in your brother's eye and pay no attention to the plank in your own eye?
4 How can you say to your brother, `Let me take the speck out of your eye,' when all the time there is a plank in your own eye?
5 You hypocrite, first take the plank out of your own eye, and then you will see clearly to remove the speck from your brother's eye.

Children of God need to start spending as much time on their spiritual wardrobe and spiritual attributes and they do on their physical ones. When we began to do this, God's beauty will definitely show in each of us and

57

will be more visible to those who view us.

Take some time to do a spiritual makeover and let God's glory show through you. When you look at yourself through the eyes of the Father, I guarantee, you will not be depressed, but rejoice in the beauty of God's perfect creation, which is you.

Submitting To The Will of God

We often want things in life, and we want immediate gratification. We get upset when we can't have those things that we want right now. We want the new job, the new car, and new house, among other things.

Do you ever wonder why even though the bible says that God answers prayer, we often don't get the things we want or think we deserve?

Oftentimes our wants and desires don't line up with the will of God. God provides us with the desires of our hearts, according to his will. We have to be willing to submit to the will of God, even if it means sacrificing those things that we want.

Sometimes God does give us the desires of our hearts and once we have those things that we have requested, we forget about the ultimate provider. God will sometimes provide you with the things that you want to see if you will utilize them to further His kingdom. But remember, just as he gave it to you, he can take it from you if it is not used appropriately.

When you get that new job with the higher salary, do you increase your giving in your offering? When you get that new house, do you invite God in? When you get that new car, how often to you take it to church an offer to bring someone with you?

In order for us to prosper, we have to live our lives according to God's will and God's word. Living according to His will may mean giving up some of those things that you hold near and dear to your heart. You may have to give up that friend who you have known for years, but he or she is not a positive influence in your life. You may have to give up that relationship where your significant other is not walking with God. You may have to walk away from a job and take a pay decrease because the place where you are employed is working against the kingdom of God.

Submitting to the will of God is not easy, but the increase is definitely worth it. When your life lines up with the will of God, you will be blessed beyond measure. You will have a new walk. Your conversation will be different. Your social circle will change and your life will be better in every aspect.

When you submit to the will of God, people will look at you and see God in you. When people talk to you, they will hear God speak through you and when people come in contact with you, God will touch their lives also.

Inner Peace

Peace is commonly understood to mean the absence of hostilities. Other definitions include freedom from disputes, silence, harmonious relations, or inner contentment and serenity as the meaning of the word changes with context.

Peace can be an emotion or internal state. And finally, peace can be any combination of these definitions. In looking at the definition of peace, how does one attain spiritual peace? We could start by letting go of those past hurts and hostilities towards others. We cannot grow spiritually if we are carrying years' worth of past grudges with us every day of our lives.

We could also begin by working to resolve those inner conflicts that we have going on within ourselves. Let go of the notion that you are not good enough, just because people have said that to you or made you feel that way all of your life. Our Father created us in him image and we are good because God does not make mistakes. Just because someone tells you that you will never amount to anything does not make it so. The word of God says in Jeremiah 29:11- God says, "For I know the plans I have for you; plans not to harm you but to prosper you. Plans to give you hope and a future".

We could learn to trust and believe that God will keep the promises that He has made to us, as He is not man

and does not lie. His word says to cast our cares upon Him because He cares for us. If we turn our burdens over to the Lord, we can attain peace.
Coming in contact with the Lord and being in His presence is also a source of the greatest peace. Allowing Him into your heart will fill you with tranquility beyond measure.

The word states in Philippians 4:6-7 6 Do not be anxious about anything, but in everything, by prayer and petition, with thanksgiving, present your requests to God. 7And the peace of God, which transcends all understanding, will guard your hearts and your minds in Christ Jesus.

It is written and because God said it, it is true.

Love

What is love? What does it truly mean? Has anyone ever acquired true love? The word of God in I Corinthians 13: 1-8 states:

1 Suppose I speak in the languages of human beings and of angels. If I don't have love, I am only a loud gong or a noisy cymbal. 2 Suppose I have the gift of prophecy. Suppose I can understand all the secret things of God and know everything about him. And suppose I have enough faith to move mountains. If I don't have love, I am nothing at all. 3 Suppose I give everything I have to poor people. And suppose I give my body to be burned. If I don't have love, I get nothing at all. 4 Love is patient. Love is kind. It does not want what belongs to others. It does not brag. It is not proud. 5 It is not rude. It does not look out for its own interests. It does not easily become angry. It does not keep track of other people's wrongs. 6 Love is not happy with evil. But it is full of joy when the truth is spoken. 7 It always protects. It always trusts. It always hopes. It never gives up. 8 Love never fails. But prophecy will pass away. Speaking in languages that had not been known before will end. And knowledge will pass away.

If you look at what the word says about love, you have to wonder why so many love relationships fail. The answer to that is rather easy...we are human!

Parental Love

God blesses us with the privilege of being parents. I say that it is a privilege because you have those who really want children, but for one reason or another are unable to conceive and give birth.

He gives us charge over these young lives so that they can become the future leaders of His kingdom. All that we impart in our children should be for the glory of the Lord.

As parents, we love our children. Even when they are being disobedient and are doing things that are not pleasing in our sight, we still love them. When our children fall by the wayside, as parents, we are usually there to pick them up and help them get back on their feet.

We teach them, care for them and love them and pray that when they are older, they values that we have placed in them will carry over into their lives. The word of God says in Proverbs 22:6 Train up a child in the way he should go, Even when he is old he will not depart from it.

Even though our children sometimes detour from the path that we have set forth for them, we still love them.

Our children can sometimes do things that are so hurtful and disappointing to us, but as parents we forgive them and we continue to provide them with love.

Isn't it amazing how the love we have for our children is a direct reflection of the love that our Father has for us? We do things in our everyday lives that man may not forgive us for, but our Father in heaven forgives us over and over again.

No matter how bad we mess up in our lives, our Father continues to shower us with His love and understanding. His love for us is so great that He sent His son to die for our sins. This is an example of the ultimate parental love.

When you feel that no one else on this earth loves you, know that your Father in heaven is there and he loves you. He has always loved you and he always will.

Your Spiritual Health

How is your health? In asking this question of someone, the natural response would be for them to respond according to their physical health. They will tell you of their aliments, physicians' visits and every medication that they take.

Depending on the age of the individual in question, the length of the answer will vary from the short "I am doing well, thank you", to an extremely detailed accounting of every single symptom, ache and pain that they are experiencing.

Almost all of us have a particular physician that we see when we are having issues with our physical or even mental health. We are willing to recommend the people who have given us satisfactory service to our families and friends. Sometimes we turn to the old home remedies of our parents, grandparents and maybe even older ancestors. You know, the tried and true home remedy that has never failed. But let me ask you, who do we turn to when we are experiencing difficulties with our spiritual health?

I have a recipe that will help to heal your spirit and keep it healthy, as long as you follow the directions. The recipe is as follows:

Take a dose of vitamin GOD every day of your life.

There is never a danger of an overdose, so take it as often as you need it.

Have yourself a big helping of Jesus. I recommend keeping of full cup of Him with you all day every day. Drink in the word of God. It doesn't matter how much you take in, but make sure that you have some every day.

Add a dose of faith. You don't need much. Faith the size of a mustard seed is enough to sustain you.

Add some of prayer into the mix. If you are a babe in Christ it's okay to start with a little. You can always add more later.

Take a walk at least once a week to the house of the Lord.

In case of emergency, you can always run to His throne.

This recipe can put you on the right path to getting yourself spiritually fit. Once your spirit is in shape, it is important for you to maintain it. Fellowshipping with others who are spiritually fit or striving to be is a wonderful way of keeping your spirit in shape. There is nothing like a group of people working toward the same goal to provide you with motivation.

The Responsibility of Being Blessed

Many of us pray for blessings for our loved ones, our friends and ourselves. I wonder how many people have ever taken the time to consider their responsibility in requesting and receiving a blessing from the Lord.

When we go before the Lord and ask for a specific blessing, we expect to receive it. We as children of God have a distinct responsibility upon receiving a blessing from the Father. He does not bless us for us. He blesses us so that we can go out and be a blessing to someone else.

I wonder how many of us have prayed for a blessing, received it and forgotten where our blessings come from. How many of us have blocked future blessings by squandering the ones that we have already received?

I am reminded of a story of a person who was down on their luck. They lost their job and was very close to being homeless. They was literally depending on the kindness of others for their survival. I remember ministering to that person and telling them that they needed to pray for what they wanted and to be obedient to the word of God.

This person starting to pray and eventually their prayers were answered and they were blessed with a job and a very good salary. I asked the person had they thanked God for their blessing and if they'd gone to church yet. They stated that they were looking into churches in the area and that they would attend. I reminded them that they needed to remember where their blessing came from and to acknowledge the source.

At the current time, this person is unemployed (less than a year after receiving this blessing) and having to relocate. Imagine how different their life would be if they'd only used their blessing the way God intended.

Let me ask you, how are you using the blessings that have been bestowed upon you? Are you in turn being a blessing to someone else, or are you keeping it all to yourself? Have you told anyone of the goodness of the Lord or do you feel that everything you have received has been obtained by you and you alone? The answer to this question should be evident in your everyday living.

As a Christian who has been blessed by the Lord, please do the responsible thing: acknowledge the source of your blessings, thank Him for the blessings and go out and be a blessing in the life of another one of God's children.

My Story

When my innocence was being stolen
At the tender age of eight
And angel came down
Stopped the torture
And led me safely home
Lord, I knew it was you

There was a time, in the not so distant past, when children were allowed to be children. Back in the day, we are able to play outside, hang out with our friends and just be children. I really enjoyed just being a child. That all changed for me in the matter of one day.

When I was eight years old, I remember my mother sending me to the store to pick up some things for her. The store was just around the corner from where we lived, and I used to go all the time, so it was no big deal for me to go on this day. Or so I thought.

As I was walking in the direction of the store, I noticed a man walking toward me. He was looking at the addresses on the buildings in what appeared to be an attempt to find a particular address. Little did I know that this was not the case.

I continued to walk past this person assuming that he was going to continue past me and keep going. Well, I was wrong. This adult male put a knife to my throat and told me if I screamed he would kill me.

I am sure that you can imagine the terror that overcame me at that point. I was obedient and did not scream for fear that he would carry out his threat. He then took me into the outer basement of one of the apartment buildings and forced me to perform sexual acts.

I remember asking him if he was going to kill me, and him not responding. I recall asking him why he was doing this and again I received no response. This torture went on for what seemed like hours, but in reality, it was less than one hour.

In the middle of this horrible ordeal, a little girl came down the stairs, looked into the basement and simply stated, "I see you" and left. My attacker ran from the basement and did not return.

It took me a while to move because I was frozen with fear. I didn't know if he was coming back to finish what he'd started. A few minutes passed and I got myself together and ran home.

The little girl that I mentioned was not someone that I'd ever seen before, and I never saw her again. Living on the block, I knew all of the children, but she was completely unfamiliar to me.

I felt then as I do now, that she was an angel sent by God to bring me out of that situation and get me home safely.

After I got home and told my mother what happened, the police were called. During the course of their investigation, they went to the building and inquired about the little girl who came to my rescue. No one knew who she was.

I know in my heart of hearts that she was my guardian angel ad I thank God for her.

When the gangs tried to recruit me
And wanted to do me bodily harm
Because I would not conform
I got home safely
Each and every day
Lord, I know that it was you

Eighth grade is supposed to be a very happy time in the life of a young person. It is the time of a major transition. You should be looking forward to your eighth grade luncheon, getting your autograph book singed by your friends, graduation and moving on to high school. What an exciting time in the life of a young person

When I was in eighth grade, I did look forward to all of those things. I was excited about the opportunities that lie ahead of me and I was anxious to move on. It was a very happy time for me, as long as I was inside the walls of the school.

Growing up on the Westside of Chicago at the time that I was in eighth grade, we started to develop some serious problems with gangs in the neighborhood, and you never knew who was going to be the target.

It was nothing like the gang activity that we see today, with all the senseless killings, innocent victims of drive by shootings, turf wars and drug dealers, not only on the corners, but also in the classroom. At that time you were relatively safe inside the school walls.

The problem that I experienced was the walk to and from school. I looked a lot younger than I actually was, so the gangs wanted to recruit me. Their rationale was that because I looked young and innocent, I could steal and get away with it. Can you imagine that? They wanted me in a gang, not because I was tough, but because of my appearance.

When I refused to participate in their activities, they started in with their intimidation tactics. They would follow me and threaten to take my coat and shoes. They would push me around and once a female gang member hit me hard enough to daze me.

After this incident, some of the girls in the building where I lived started walking to school with me. Eventually the gang members got it through their head that I was not going to change my mind, so they moved on to another target.

I thank God for giving me the strength to not be intimidated into doing the things that the gangs would have me do. I also thank Him for putting people in place to ensure my safe commute to and from school

I pray that more of our young people realize sooner
rather than later that the gang life is really no life at all.
There is not positive future in gang activity. The
possible outcomes are injury, prison or death. Those are
not the plans that God has for his children.

When peers tried to pressure me
Into doing things that I knew were wrong
I was able to stand my ground,
Say no, that's not for me
Graduate high school with no real problems
Lord, I know that it was you

High school! What a glorious, fun filled time! This is the
time for a person to start really forming their identity
and aligning themselves with people who have the
potential to become lifelong friends. It is also a time
when young people get to make more decisions that
could affect their future. It is a time of choices.

I had friends in high school that chose to smoke, drink,
have sex (sometimes in school) and do drugs. I chose
not to engage in those behaviors and was excluded from
a lot of activities because of it.

Because I chose not to engage in those particular
activities, I got through school without some of the
consequences that they had to face, such as parent
conferences about behavior, suspension and expulsion.

Now I am not claiming that I was an angel in high school. I, like many teenaged girls, went through some major attitude problems. If I didn't like something or someone, I made it known. I also had the occasional fight with a fellow student. There were times when we were dismissed early and I would go to the mall with one of my friends instead of going straight home, but nothing to the extent of some of the behaviors that I was aware of then and nothing close to what I witness young people doing today.

I thank God for blessing me with parents who taught me about making wise choices (either out of good judgment or fear). I believe the choices I made then helped to mold the person that I am, and that I am becoming.

When I was able to get an apartment
Work two jobs while going to school
Keep the bills and the rent paid
Keep food on the table
Not fall over from exhaustion
Lord, I knew it was you

Being grown isn't easy. Don't ever let anyone tell you that it is. How many times do you remember saying "I can't wait until I get grown and on my own"? I bet if you knew then what you know now, you would eat those words!

I have been on my own since I was nineteen years old. I had my own apartment, got a job and was going to school. I had a roommate for a while, but that didn't work out and she moved back home with her family.

Living on my own as a young woman was not easy. Trying to work to pay the bills and buy food while going to school was very difficult and there were times when I didn't think I was going to make it.

From time to time, I had to turn to my parents for assistance. This was very difficult for me because as my father would say, I was independent to a fault. They never denied me assistance when needed, but I didn't want to have to ask.

I have a friend who lived down the street at the time and we were having similar struggles. She and I would float $10-$20 between us to help each other get by. This was also during the time of the paper food stamps. We would get our stamps, pool our resources and go shopping. We lived on liver cheese and crackers, cans of ravioli, chips, soda and whatever else we could afford with our limited resources. We are still friends to this day.

I remember losing my job at one point and not knowing how I was going to make ends meet. The bills were coming in, but the money was not. I recall asking the Lord for help, and don't you know he came through! I had been waiting for some money to come in, but it had not yet arrived. I remember not checking my mailbox on a Saturday because I just didn't want to look at any more bills. I checked my mailbox the next day and there were the two checks that I'd been waiting for. I had enough money to cover the rent, bills and buy food. The Lord is good!

During this time, I registered with a temp agency so that I could have some money coming in, just until I found a steady job. I was blessed with some long-term assignments, pretty steady pay and was able to stay afloat financially. One of my final assignments with this agency was to work in the customer service department of a local firm. The assignment was scheduled to last six weeks. Two and a half years later I was released from that assignment. During my time with this company, I completed my bachelor's degree, got married and had my first child.

God certainly saw me through some very trying times as a single young woman and he continues to see me through every trial and tribulation. For that, I thank Him.

When my friend stopped speaking to me
Because I was not ready to accept
What he wanted to offer me
And then he returned
And became my husband
Lord, I know that it was you

Did you ever have that one friend who you could always count on, no matter what? You know, that friend who was there for you through all of your personal drama and all of your dating drama? The friend, who stood by you, advised you and never judged you?

I had a friend like that. He would let me complain and whine and he was always there. He never told me that he didn't want to hear it; he just let me vent.

One day after one of my venting sessions over the most recent boyfriend, I told him that I was giving up on dating. He asked me "what about me?" That was something that I did not expect. As a matter of fact, it was something that I never even thought of. Without taking the time to think about it, I told him no. I told him that I could not date him because he was my friend. Who dates their friends, right?

I wish that I had realized then that friendship should be at the very foundation of any relationship. Maybe, had I realized this, I would not have had so much drama in my personal life.

Anyway, because of my lack of judgment, my friend walked out of my life. I didn't hear from him for nearly two years. I would call him and he would not respond. He made no attempt to reach out to me at all.

You know that old saying "you never know what you have until it's gone"? Well, that is a very true statement. I didn't realize how much I could miss a person until he stopped communicating with me. There is another saying that goes "you can't see what you have right in front of you". This is another very true statement. All of the qualities that I was looking for in a mate, I had in my friend and didn't realize it until it were too late, or so I thought.

One day, out of the blue, he called me. At the time, I had gotten involved in yet another unproductive relationship, which I ended the very moment I hung up the phone with my friend. I had no idea where things were going to go with us, but I didn't want anything to interfere with whatever was to come.

Three years after that phone call we were married. Twenty two years later we are still together. This just goes to show that sometimes you have to get out of your own way and let God have his way. Lesson taught. Lesson learned!

When a life growing inside of me
Was taken away in the womb
Because it was not strong enough
To survive in the outside world
I was able to have peace of mind
Lord, I know it was you

Pregnancy is supposed to be a time of great hope, joy, excitement, anticipation and expectation in the life of a family. When a woman learns that she has been blessed with the gift of life growing inside of her, it should be one of the greatest moments in her life.

Most women, upon finding out that they are pregnant, immediately move into what I like to call "mommy mode". The begin picturing what their child will look like and all of the things that the child can achieve in life. It is a most glorious time.

Now imagine having that great joy turn into an equal or greater sorrow when during a visit to the physician the mother is told that the baby is not growing, there is no heartbeat and it must be removed from her womb.

Suddenly all of the joy is gone from you and your life changes for what, in that moment, seems like forever.

Any woman who has ever experienced the loss of a child knows that it causes a pain so great that it hurts you to your very soul. This is a pain and sorry that I know from personal experience. In that moment I knew that nothing would ever be the same again. And it wasn't.

I had a talk with God and He told me that everything was going to be alright because He was in control. My tears stopped and I developed a great sense of peace. No one around me could understand how I could be so calm following such a traumatic experience. I simply said to them "God knew what was best". It didn't matter what anyone else thought because I knew that the Master was in control.

When you are struggling with a situation from which you think that you may never recover, just remember that as long as you have God on your side, you will make it through.

Because of experiencing the loss of a child, I feel that it

enables me to appreciate my children more. If I didn't
know the feeling of losing a child, I would probably not
experience the abundant joy that my children bring me
in the way that I experience it. Without the pain of
loss, I would have taken the joy for granted. Thank God
for the lessons that He has taught me.

When going through
The illness of pregnancy
The pain of labor
And giving birth to
Two beautiful, healthy children
Lord, I know that it was you

Many women that I know had a wonderful pregnancy
experience. They had that healthy pregnant glow. They
were able to eat whatever they wanted and some even
experienced a surge in their energy level. I had women
tell me that being pregnant was the healthiest and
happiest time in their lives. That is so not my story!

Pregnancy, for me, was the most difficult time in my life.
I have heard people say that every pregnancy is
different, but in my case, my pregnancies were identical.

My pregnancies consisted of numerous trips to the
emergency room, multiple hospitalizations, being
unable to eat, significant weight loss (60 pounds with
each child) being fed through and IV and a lot of time
off work. My pregnancies had my entire family stressed
out. I remember my mother telling me "When you are
pregnant, the whole family is pregnant".

I was in the ER so often that I knew all of the doctors by name and when each doctor was on shift. This went on for the first six months of my pregnancy.

My doctors were concerned about my weight loss with both pregnancies because they were not certain how my weight loss would affect the baby. Both children were over six pounds.

With my first child, labor was painful, but it was quick. She was born in five hours, perfectly healthy. I have heard people say that the second child comes faster than the first. Again, not my story! My second child took twelve hours and I had to get an epidural to deal with the pain, something I didn't have to do with my first child.

Out of all of the pain and suffering I endured, God blessed me with two beautiful and healthy children, which proves that God won't give you more than you can handle.

Out of my agony came such beauty and I thank God for the blessings that he has given me in my children.

When my child was stolen
And in the care of strangers
With prayer, she was returned safely
Clean and not hungry
No harm came to her
Lord, I know that it was you

Each of us have gone through some things in our lives, and we didn't know how we were going to make it through, but somehow, whatever our situation, it worked out. It was nothing less than the power of God working out a situation for us that we could not fix for ourselves.

I am a witness to the power of God in my own life. I have been placed in some situations where I didn't know how I was going to make it, but God showed up and brought me out. I created some of the situations, and others were the work of the adversary.

I would like to give a personal testimony about the goodness of God and how He brought my family through a situation.

On Wednesday morning, February 17, 1999, my husband left to take our two daughters aged 4 and 14 months to their respective child care providers. About ten minutes after they left, I received a call from my husband telling me that the car had been stolen, the baby was inside and he simply said "Start praying".

As a parent, one of the most horrible things imaginable is having your child taken and not knowing who has them. It is a situation that leaves one feeling completely helpless. But I know from whence cometh my help.

As my husband requested, I started praying as I got myself prepared to go to the place where the car was stolen. Not only did I pray, but I called everyone that I thought could get a prayer through, and requested that they pray also.

Four hours later, my husband's car was located in the parking lot of a nearby police station. My daughter was inside the vehicle. The keys were left in the ignition and the registration was placed where it could be seen. Her diaper had been changed and she had been fed. She had not been harmed in any way.

People commented that I remained too calm during that entire ordeal. My response to them was "I knew that God would not let anything happen to my baby. He did not bless me with this child to have her taken away from me".

People also questioned if I was upset with my husband for leaving her in the car unattended. My response was that no one is perfect. He made a mistake. I requested that people not judge him or speak out against him because of it. No one has the right to judge him but God.

God brought my child safely through that situation and has kept my family together. He never puts you in a situation that he cannot bring you out of. That situation could have ended horribly, as we know these things sometimes do, but when you have faith and believe and call on the name of Jesus, he will bring you out. To God be the glory!

When people placed in authority over me
Have made my life a living hell
I made a change in my attitude
To be able to work with them
And get the job done
Lord, I know that it was you

Every one of us has had or will have some person in a position of authority over us who believes that their job description is to make our lives as miserable as possible for as long as possible.

Some people take the power given to them by man for granted and use it as an excuse to be mean to others. I remember having one employer telling me she didn't have to be nice because she was the boss. I explained to her that because she was the boss, she needed to be nice because she could not run the place alone.

I have worked with people who believe that they could do or say anything they wanted to me and it was my job to accept it. These people used to make me so angry and have me so upset that I would often make myself sick.

After a while I realized that when you let people make you that angry or upset, they have power over you. Once I realized this, I changed the way that I responded to their behavior. I learned that I could not control their behavior, but I could control my own.

When they would get mean, I would respond by being

extra nice. When they were rude, it made me more polite. I noticed that when I changed my response to their treatment of me, it made them angry. They could not understand why I was not upset.

I was not upset because I was keenly aware the God had the ultimate control over my life and that people could only treat me as bad as I allowed them. When I started to take my power back, they tried to find ways to get rid of me. Their attempts were futile because God was in control of my situation. The word of God says in Psalm 105:15 "Do not touch My anointed ones, and do My prophets no harm." When you are one of God's children, the plans of the enemy are sure to fail.

I worked at a company for about four years with a lady who was cruel just to be cruel. She would walk into the office and no one knew who her target was going to be that day. She would yell, scream and throw things. You just never knew what to expect from her.

She called me in one day and told me that she was going to have to lay me off because she could no longer afford to pay me and that I had two weeks left to work. At another time in my life I would have been really upset, but I knew that God would take care of me.

I immediately went back into my office and started sending out resumes. Before the end of the day, I had two interviews set up. As I was leaving for the day, she said to me, laughingly, "I know it is going to be hard, but try to have a good evening". I turned and looked at her and told her that it was going to be a great evening and that I would be late the next day because I had an interview. The look on her face was nothing less than priceless.

In another job, I worked with people who did not believe and God and would condemn you for being a Christian. My immediate supervisor would deliberately do things to attempt to upset me or throw me off task, but I would not let her succeed. She would be sexually inappropriate with me and get upset when her advances were not returned. Because she felt as though I rejected her, she did everything possible to make things difficult for me. But I had a joy that she could not steal. That's what happens when God gets on the inside of you. People cannot steal the things that God has given you.

Through all of the criticism, extra work, write ups and other attempts to break my spirit, I walked through the office singing, smiling and praising God. God then told me that it was okay for me to leave that place and I started preparing myself for the blessings that I knew was coming for me.

I remember cleaning out my desk in January and preparing for a job that God had not given me yet. I continued to do my job as well as sing and praise the Lord. One day I was called into the office to be written up for something that my supervisor asked me to do and then subsequently denied. I signed the write up, walked out and smiled. Within a few days I got a call with an offer for a job.

I clearly remember the day that I turned in my resignation. I gave a copy to my supervisor and her boss. He read it and declared "You're quitting?! You got a job?!" I told him that the Lord provided and it was time for me to go. He turned a shade of red that I had never seen in a human being.

When you let God lead you and you are obedient to him, he will give you just what you need when you need it the most. If you put your faith in Him, He will never let you down.

When my friend was taken
In the prime of his life
Because he was suffering
You saw fit to call him home
Though I miss him dearly
Lord, I know that it was you

One of the hardest things in the world is to suddenly lose someone that you care about. It's hard even when you know that they are ill and suffering, but when you are unaware of their situation, it makes it harder.

I had a person in my life, who did not start out as a friend, but grew to be one, and he was called home by God at a very young age.

This is a person who, when he entered my life, I truly disliked. Not because of who he was, but because of the way he entered my life. He was my choir director and he replaced a choir director that we had and really liked. And again, it is not that he replaced her, it was the manner in which it was done.

This person was very passionate about his music and he sometimes came across as mean. He was hard on us because he knew our potential and he was pulling the best out of us. A lot of people in the choir did not understand him and did not like him because of his teaching methods and feedback.

I was a person who was very insecure in my singing ability (and to a degree I still am). He pushed me and worked with me until I became a little more confident in my abilities. He said that he saw something in me that needed to be brought out and he was determined to bring it out.

I took the time to get to know him as a person, not just a diligent choir director, and we became friends. Even after he left our church to pursue other ventures, we kept in touch.

One day we received an announcement at church that he was in the hospital in the intensive care unit. After church, me and another choir member went to the hospital to see him but he had so many visitors that we were not allowed to see him that day.

I went back the next day and was allowed to go up to visit with him. I had not seen him in a while because he was on tour doing a play, and the person that I saw when I went into that hospital room was a mere shadow of the man that I had known. He was so thin. It took all of my strength to hold back the tears. Fortunately, there was another member of the church there and that kept me grounded.

After she left, he and I talked for a while longer and it appeared that he was getting tired. I asked him if he wanted to lie down and he said no, he wanted to finish telling me his story. He was bearing his soul about a lot of past hurts and regrets and he wanted to get it all out. He stated that he never knew how many people really loved him until he got sick. He stated that he was very grateful to all that came to visit him, pray with him and fellowship with him during his illness. He was determined that he was going to get better so that he could finish his tour with the play.

During that visit, he had a stroke. I ran from the room to get help because I didn't know what was going on with him. The nurses came and put him to bed and after that; he was unable to verbally communicate. I saw him a few times after that and then he was moved to a hospice facility. He died a couple of weeks later.

When I got the call that he'd gone home to be with God, I wasn't as upset as I thought that I would be. I saw how ill he was and how he suffered. I was relieved to know that his suffering had ended. My only regret was that I was unable to attend his funeral. I did, however, have a chance to say goodbye prior to him get going to hospice.

There are times when I will hear a song that he directed or sang and it brings a smile to my face. I can see him jumping around or fussing at us to "focus" and it makes me chuckle.

I thank God for the blessing of allowing me to know him for the short time that I did and for the happy memories that I carry with me.

When people have been placed in my life
The good ones have remained
And become great friends
The wrong ones were revealed
And subsequently removed
Lord, I know that it was you

Most of us have heard the statement that God puts people in your life for a reason and for a season. Many people don't believe that or don't understand it. Some people are placed in your life so that you can learn something from the experience of having known them.

Not all of those lessons are meant to be positive ones, but God will use the means that He sees necessary to reveal what you need to know. You might not understand it at the time that the lesson is being taught, but God means it for your good.

People that you have been friends with for a long time may not be meant to be friends for a lifetime. There are people that I have known for many years, with whom

God has told me that I need to sever the relationship.

I have had friends whom when I was doing things that were against the will of God, encouraged the bad behavior. God told me that I had to let them go and I did.

There are other people in my life who have been there through the good and the bad and are still around. They have encouraged me to grow in a positive manner and have been very supportive. I have tried to reciprocate the encouragement and support.

There have been people that I have allowed into my lie for all of the wrong reasons and the relationships were completely unhealthy. God gave me the strength and the wisdom to walk away and not let those relationships destroy my life.

God will surround you with those people who will keep you on the right path, we just have to take off our human eyes, view them with our spiritual eyes so that we will be able to ascertain who is there for our good and who is not.

Through all that I have endured
Whether good and pleasant
Or a learning experience
That I managed to survive
I know that I am better for them all
Lord, because it was you

I could go on and on about how God had moved through my life and made a difference, but if I did, my story would never end. He reveals himself to me in different ways every day and I am just thankful for every day that I have with Him. Even when I don't understand what it is He is trying to show me, I know that He would never harm me and that in all things He is there for me.

I have to take the time to tell Him that I love Him, I adore Him, I honor Him and I bless His holy name for without Him I am nothing. I thank Him for every blessing that he has bestowed upon me and every lesson ever taught.

I thank Him for keeping me from all hurt harm and danger and for blessing me with the gifts that he has given me.

Isn't it great to serve a God who takes care of you day after day, whether you deserve it or not?

Thank you Father for loving me!

Text & Images Copyright
Crystal Wilson-Honesty, 2016

Made in the USA
Middletown, DE
17 August 2016